What others ar

Edie Melson is a trustworthy source to write a book on soul care for women. She's a woman of great faith that's poured out in prayer, great creativity that is revealed in both her publishing and photography endeavors, and great love that translates into caring for and encouraging others. All three of these characteristics prompted Edie to write *Soul Care When You're Weary*—a valuable resource for women today.

~Beth K. Vogt, Christy award-winning author

Are you overwhelmed and exhausted? Your body may actually be sending signals that deep within you have neglected your soul. But Honey, you are worth restoration and renewal – beginning today! Edie Melson's new *Soul Care When You're Weary* is both an inspirational and practical handbook to help realign all those places in your life that have gone off kilter—your focus, your health, your emotions, your creativity, and your relationship with God. Inside these pages is a treasure chest of devotions, creative exercises, journaling, scripture and more. Don't tackle everything at once. Take these words in small doses and discover a fresh new world of fulfillment and joy.

~Lucinda Secrest McDowell, author of *Dwelling Places* and *Ordinary Grace*s

In the pages of this book, Edie Melson stopped me in my tracks, made me take a look at my frenzied pace and admit my soul fatigue. Then before I knew it, she took my hand and helped me find rest and joy. This book will become dog-eared and dear, its pages filled with my soul's meanderings as Edie guides me through my weariness and beyond to

joy! *Soul Care When You're Weary* is an oasis for all whose creativity has been taken captive by busyness and anxiety.
~Audrey Frank, author of Instead of Shame...
Honor, Harvest House Publishers, August 2019

Edie Melson's *Soul Care When You're Weary* inspired me to look deeper into the creative spirit that God had gifted me and embrace His presence in every aspect of my life. This devotional is a keeper.
~DiAnn Mills, best-selling author

Life often brings avalanche-like circumstances in which you can find overwhelming weariness. A remedy often prescribed today is to focus on health and wellness physically to get back on track. Although this is important, there is a weariness that roots itself below the physical, the kind of tiredness that hits the core of our personhood. *Soul Care When You're Weary*, speaks to a different type of remedy for weariness, one that goes beyond taking a nap or making healthy choices physically. Edie beautifully extends an invitation to walk down a path to engage creativity that fosters intimacy with God to refresh the soul. Each chapter is designed as a guide to take care of your soul through inspirational devotions rich with scripture, practical exercises of creativity (even if you don't think you are creative) and prayers that encourage intimacy with God.
~Cynthia Cavanaugh-Speaker, Life Coach, and author
of *Anchored: Leading Through the Storms*

Edie goes beyond moving words and asks us to act upon them. Rich in texture and meaningful responses to the inquiries we often ask of God, it is in these pages we see our hands at work, and find His voice.
~Vanessa Denniston, artist and writer

Soul Care When You're Weary

Edie Melson

Bold Vision Books
PO Box 2011
Friendswood, Texas 77549

Dedication

This book is gratefully dedicated to

My Mother,

Monita Mahoney

You taught me to embrace the creative legacy

passed down from you and Daddy.

Then you set me on my journey

with encouraging words and lots of love.

Table of Contents

Chapter Three—Reconnecting with Prayer Play

Acknowledgments

No book can ever see the light of day without an entire team of people moving it forward. That's especially true of this book.

First and foremost, I want to give a shout-out to my amazing husband, Kirk Melson. Without his constant support and encouragement—as well as his willingness to chip in with almost everything around the house—this book would not have happened.

I also want to thank those in my life who have given this project, and all of us involved, much needed—daily—prayer support. Cathy Baker, Candace Brady, Sheri Owens, Valorie Moore, Vonda Skelton, Beth Vogt, and Cynthia Cavanaugh. I also want to thank my Friday morning, More Than Sunday, accountability group. You guys are an inspiration. And I could never leave out my precious critique partners Lynette Eason, Alycia Morales, Lynn Blackburn, Linda Gilden, Erynn Newman, Emme Gannon, and Mary Denman.

A special shout out goes to my amazing (and in my opinion best) agent in the world, David Van Diest.

Of course I want to include everyone at Bold Vision Books. You are the greatest group any author could ever hope to be blessed with.

Additionally, no writer is ever able to move ahead without other writers to share the journey. Thank you to all the writers from my AWSA Mastermind Group, Cross N Pens, ACFW SC Chapter, and of course The Light Brigade.

Finally a *huge* shout out to my sons and daughters, Jimmy and Katie Melson, Kirk and Weslyn Melson, and John Melson. You all have always believed in me and been among my staunchest supporters. I love doing life with you all.

Introduction

The world around us is continuing to spiral out of control. Our lives are busier and the margin we have available for recovery and peace is shrinking. As we struggle to cope and search for answers, we've neglected the legacy of creativity that's been passed to us from our Heavenly Father. This legacy isn't frivolous. It's foundational for the deep relationship with God we all need.

We see the people yearning for time to rest and reconnect across every level of society as the Bible journaling and coloring book market has exploded. At the heart of that popularity is our need to play, fueled by the fact that we've forgotten the importance of exercising our creativity in order to maintain the health of our souls.

Sensory involvement can deepen our relationship with our Father and give rest to weary souls. God's strength—for every circumstance—sometimes flows best when we open the creative channels in our souls.

When we're hurting and the stress of the world presses in, we need to be reminded that God is still the answer. He's always present, and He cares deeply about every aspect of our lives, even as He works to bring good from bad.

This book addresses our drive to reconnect with the tactile creativity that lies dormant. I grew up in a household of creatives—my mother is an internationally known artist and my father was a classically trained musician and photographer. Connecting to God through creativity has been a cornerstone of my life—especially when challenges arise.

I know what it's like to let God's power flow through creativity. I've dealt with the struggles of life while clinging to God. Now I'm using my insight to help others find that connection with God—through creativity—when stress is high and time is short.

My desire is for this book to be something you can use. My prayer is that it will be become dog-eared and stained from carrying it around. I urge you to draw in it, experiment, and learn once again the healing power of play—especially play with our Heavenly Father.

You can use this book with nothing more than a pen or pencil. But if you want to go further, here is a list of supplies you might enjoy using.

Optional Supply List

- Colored Pencils
- Markers, fine tip, brush, and/or glitter
- Paint, acrylic and/or watercolor
- Washi Tape
- Stickers
- Gelato sticks
- Glue
- Glitter
- Ribbon

In addition, there are several instances where I encourage you to take a photograph. You don't need special equipment.

- Cell phone camera
- An Instamatic of some kind, like Fujifilm Instax or Polaroid Snap
- Digital camera

Chapter One—*Triage*

When we're weary, we need immediate relief. Unfortunately the activities and emotions that sap our energy, also make it difficult for us to dig deep into God's Word to find that relief. We're not looking for a shortcut. What we need is a way to connect with God's presence without adding to burdens we're already carrying.

God has a plan for that.

He's made a provision for our need of rest by ordaining a time of Sabbath as a part of our regular routine, so we know that taking time to let go is a priority in His plan for us. But we've forgotten what it's like to play. We've turned recreation into work. Or worse yet, labeled fun as something unnecessary and frivolous.

In this chapter, we'll begin identifying some of the stresses that are triggering the weariness you're facing, and some of the ways God has already set into motion as the antidote for that bone-deep feeling of exhaustion.

And we'll do it while playing as we reconnect with God's strength through creativity. There are short devotions, prayers, and lots of creativity connections to give you a chance to experience God's rest through relaxation and fun.

This book is made for play. Draw in the margins, color on top of the text. Get messy and don't be afraid to push the boundaries of creativity while you experience the rest that God has planned.

A Devotion

When We're Weary and Heavy Laden

"Come to Me, all of you who are weary and
burdened, and I will give you rest. All of
you, take up My yoke and learn from Me,
because I am gentle and humble in heart,
and you will find rest for yourselves. For
My yoke is easy and My burden is light"
(Matthew 11:28-30 HCSB).

When we're weary, the last thing we want is to take up another burden. Yet when I cried out to God begging for rest, this was the Bible verse that popped into my mind. My response wasn't that of a mature believer. It was more along the line of, "Really God? This is the best You can do?"

Not one of my better moments.

Fortunately our Father is patient and full of loving kindness. He directed me to dig deeper and dissect this passage. When I did, I found what I'd been searching for so desperately.

- The yoke is personal. In biblical times, the yoke of an ox was made from wood. It was hand carved—especially for that particular animal. It wasn't interchangeable between animals.

- The yoke is a partnership. A young, untrained ox was paired with a more mature ox that could guide and teach the young one and make his work easier.

- The yoke is perfectly fair and just. The word yoke has the same Greek root word as the balance on a scale.

God was reminding me that when I choose to go out on my own, the weight will eventually be too much. It's only when I return to His side that I'll have help with the heavy lifting.

Forging A Creative
Connection

So often when we're tired, we lose perspective.
When that happens, we can turn to God and let His
Spirit step in and lend us His eyes to see more clearly.

"Come to Me, all of you who are weary and
burdened, and I will give you rest. All of
you, take up My yoke and learn from Me,
because I am gentle and humble in heart,
and you will find rest for yourselves. For

My yoke is easy and My burden is light"
(Matthew 11:28-30 HCSB).

List all the "yokes" that you've put on yourself.
*(examples: expectations of others, perfectionist
tendencies, etc.)*

Look at what you've listed above and list how
you can move those to God's yoke
*(example: I'm trying to live up to someone else's
standards of mothering. Instead I'm going to look at
becoming more like the mother that God designed me
to be.)*

A Prayer

When Life is Overwhelming

"Jesus looked at them and said, 'With man this is impossible, but with God all things are possible'" (Matthew 19:26 NIV).

Dear Lord, You are everything I need, so why am I carrying this load alone? I have been handling my problems away from You and now I'm in trouble. I can't continue alone.

I'm ashamed to admit that I've wondered away. I know I deserve to be left alone to cope, but You promise me grace and mercy. Show me how you will work in the middle of this mess.

The stresses in my life are drowning me. I can't concentrate because of everything I have pressing in on me. I need Your priorities and Your wisdom. Speak to me through the people around and give me what I need to fix this.

Take away my fears and dry my tears. Remind me that You are the One who loves me. My faith is in You. Right now I'm acknowledging that You are all I need. Amen.

A Devotion

When You Need A Good Night's Sleep

"In peace I will lie down and sleep, for
you alone, Lord, make me dwell in safety"
(Psalm 4:8 NIV).

I rolled over, repositioned my pillow, and tried to will sleep to come. But my mind was my enemy. The thoughts crowding my brain circled like vultures, diving with sharp claws and ripping away the fabric of sleep. I couldn't pinpoint the exact source of my insomnia. There were lots of reasons for me to be stressed, but no single one appeared to be the ultimate culprit.

Finally I gave up, grabbed my Bible, and settled into the recliner downstairs where my tossing and turning wouldn't disturb my husband's rest. I thumbed through the book of Psalms, my go-to place when I'm searching for a cure, and that's when I found this Psalm highlighted.

In the past I'd used it to pray while our son was away on deployment. That night I initially dismissed it as not really relevant to my current situation and continued to skim through Scripture. When those words wouldn't leave my mind, I turned back.

Could this passage be more pertinent than I'd first thought? Two words stood out: peace and safety. Peace was definitely something I needed. Safety, however, didn't seem to fit my struggle. I couldn't pinpoint any specific fears. I prayed, asking God to share His insight.

What He answered has stayed with me. Through His Spirit's prompting, I saw that I really was afraid—of many situations. I was worried about not measuring up, not getting everything done, and not being able to continue at my current speed of life. As each fear exploded into my mind, it felt like God whispered His provision over it. As He spoke His peace, each particular worry vanished. I went through the entire list and when my mind was quiet, I was ready for sleep.

I learned that when I let fears take up residence in my mind, they grow and multiply, pushing out the peace of God.

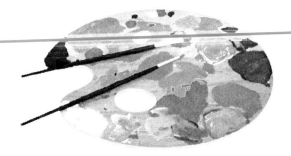

Forging A Creative Connection

Free writing can be a process of getting to the obstacles that are keeping us from the rest we so desperately need. In the space below and on the next page, write what you associate with peace. Then draw pictures, use colored pens and/or pencils, and decorate this page with stickers and Washi Tape.

_____

_____

_____

_____

A Prayer

When You Need Sleep

"If you lie down, you will not be afraid;
when you lie down, your sleep will be
sweet" (Proverbs 3:24 ESV).

Dear Lord, I'm so tired during the day, yet I can't sleep at night. My mind won't shut down. My anxious thoughts swirl into gale force winds that keep me from rest. Each day I become more weary. Lack of sleep is affecting every aspect of my life.

You promise that You'll give me the rest I need. I always thought rest was a metaphorical idea, now I desperately need to know it's a promise for the physical part of my life, too. I read how You sent angels to minister to Elijah. Please send me the help I need.

I shouldn't be this worried or this stressed. It seems like everyone I know is coping better than me. What is wrong with me? Help me remember that You designed me the way I am. Show me how to work in my strengths. Remind me that this isn't a surprise to You, and You're already at work in my life.

Even as I pray, I feel Your peace surrounding me. Why do I wait so long to come to You? You are my rock. Thank You for hearing my cry. Amen.

A Devotion

When You Need to Breathe

"God also said to Abraham, 'As for Sarai
your wife, you are no longer to call her
Sarai; her name will be Sarah'"
(Genesis 17:15 NIV).

I was weary beyond words. Circumstances piled upon circumstances had sucked all the energy from my life. I was reduced to going through the motions. I was present at work, attended family gatherings, even managed to put food on the table. It was almost too much effort to take a deep breath.

37

So often we become God's children long before we allow Him to breathe life into our lives. Our hearts belong to Him, but we often resist the changes He wants to make in us.

I think the same thing was true of Abraham and Sarah. They followed God for years before they actually let Him make the changes He wanted. These verses are the outward evidence of the changes God made in them.

The changed names held great significance. He added an H to both their names. If you say the sound that an H makes, it's an exhalation of breath— evidence that they had allowed God to breathe life into their lives.

God also breathes into us. He speaks to us in many ways. We have much more of Him than those in the Bible. We have His Holy Spirit, and we have His Living Word. But if we don't allow what God is giving us to transform us, we will never experience His rest..

Without transformation, information is extra baggage.

It's our responsibility to apply the truth God speaks. It was when I finally allowed Him to breathe into my life that I began to get a handle on the weariness of life. When we have His sustaining breath inside us, we can battle victoriously through anything.

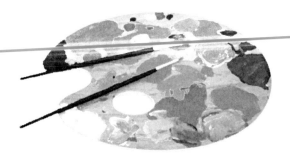

Forging A Creative Connection

The more weary we get, the narrower our focus becomes. Today, go for a walk. Even if you don't have the energy for a walk, at least step outside and look around and up. Give your soul a chance to expand into the wonderful creation all around us.

Now, record what you see and what you feel. You can take a picture with your cell phone, pluck a blade of grass or a flower. Tuck your prize into this page of the book. Let it remind you that God is still God. He's still creating beauty for us to enjoy.

Also use the space below to reproduce what you see. Draw a picture, paint a description, with words or simply use stamps and stickers to recreate what you've experienced.

A Prayer
When You're Weary

"He gives strength to the weary and
strengthens the powerless"
(Isaiah 40:29 HCSB).

Dear Lord, I'm so weary I don't know where
to start with this prayer. I want to ask for rest and
peace, but the chaos around me makes that request
seem impossible. How did my faith shrink so much?

I know that with You all things are possible.
I know You promised rest and peace, but those

promises seem to be written for someone else. Help me see You through my circumstances.

Give me something concrete that I can use as a foundation to rebuild my faith and my life. Lead others to reach out and fill in the gaps where I'm unable to cope. I know I have friends and family who want to help, but I have hesitated to reach out to them.

You are my anchor in this storm. Remind me You are always with me. Wrap Your arms around me and give me the help I need. Amen.

A Devotion

Asking God to Hold My Hand

"For I am the Lord your God who takes
hold of your right hand and says to you,
Do not fear: I will help you"
(Isaiah 41:13 NIV).

I remember the feel of my son's tiny hand in mine. And I still treasure those rare moments when his adult hand reaches out for mine. Truthfully, I've loved each stage of the hand-holding journey.

At first, his tiny baby hands would grip a single finger as I held him. Then he held tightly to me as he learned to walk. After he became more mobile, he'd hold my hand as we walked together, sometimes for balance and sometimes for reassurance. As he grew, it was more often me who insisted, "hold my hand, please." He wanted his independence and the tight connection between us cramped his style.

There were several reasons for my requests for him to hold my hand. I wanted to keep him safe and prevent him from wandering too far from me. I also could tell a lot through our physical connection. And that warm hand in mind brought me comfort because I love him so much.

As I think back on those memories, I consider my connection to my Heavenly Father. So often I hear Him whisper, "hold my hand, please."

Sometimes, when I need comfort or direction, I accept and reach out. As I find myself once again in the midst of chaos and strife, I wish I'd taken Him up on His offer sooner. It wouldn't have guaranteed that I wouldn't be where I am, but that intimate connection with Him would have given me the strength and peace I needed sooner.

So I'm going to make a deliberate effort to begin each day with my hand firmly in His, allowing Him to guide my steps, protect me from dangers I don't see, and give me the peace that can only come from Him.

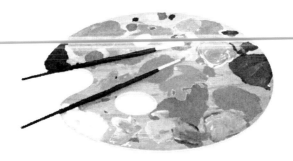

Forging A Creative Connection

When we take time to ask, God will speak to us—often in unexpected ways. Today we're going to open the door for God's revelation by playing with an acrostic. Sometimes the words in an acrostic form a sentence. In other examples, they may be lines of a poem. Or they may only be words that relate to the original word. Here's an example of an acrostic using the word, Bible:

Basic
Instruction
Before
Leaving
Earth

Make up your acrostic using the word PEACE.
Each letter can begin a single word, or you can use a
sentence with a word beginning with that letter. Get
creative and open yourself up to what God is saying
to you about PEACE. Decorate your work.

P

E

A

C

E

A Prayer

Asking For God's Strength

"Now to Him who is able to do above and beyond all that we ask or think according to the power that works in us— to Him be glory in the church and in Christ Jesus to all generations, forever and ever. Amen" (Ephesians 3:20-21 HCSB).

Dear Lord, I'm tired beyond belief and discouraged. My soul has sunk into a pit of fear and despair. I know the only way I'll ever emerge is with Your help.

Help me remember to hold tightly to You during this difficult time. I know my tendency is to focus on my circumstances. I worry about them and waste so much energy trying to find a way out—in my strength.

Protect me from myself. Use the people around me to remind me to look up. Don't let me get so exhausted that I lose all ability to reason. You are my hope. You are the light in the darkness.

Don't let me forget the times before when you've provided everything I needed—rest, peace, and answers when I didn't know the questions. You are walking through this with me. I will rely only on Your strength and then I'll praise Your name when we're through. Amen.

A Devotion

About Using Seeds of Failure to Grow Fruit

"But the fruit of the Spirit is love, joy, peace, patience, kindness, goodness, faithfulness, gentleness, self-control" (Galatians 5:22-23 NASB).

For me, this verse is tough. Some of the fruit listed are easy. Some...well...not so much.

In my travels this year, I've had the opportunity to hear about the spiritual journeys of others. I noticed most of us have a similar story. Very few have had an easy path. Instead we've all traveled a circuitous trip full of bumps and detours.

Frequently a believer's path is littered with broken dreams and shattered expectations.

As I listened to all these stories, one thing stood out. That sometimes-tortuous path made us better people. And beyond that, these twists and turns brought us face-to-face with those we could touch with the love of Jesus.

That insight made me stop to reflect on those instances in my life that I'd always labeled as failures and shortcomings. Now I see them as opportunities to grow and learn. Those times of waiting became patience, the frustration became discipline, and the rejections became joy. All those difficult circumstances had been used by God to teach me skills I lacked, as well as giving me compassion for others on similar journeys.

Somewhere along the way, God used the seeds of failure to grow fruit in my life.

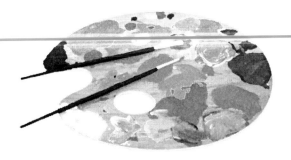

Forging a Creative
Connection

It doesn't matter what time of year it is, growing something can teach us so much. We learn patience as we wait, nurture as we care for the plant, and discipline as caring for the plant becomes a regular habit.

Today I want you to begin growing something. You can interpret this literally and plant some seeds in a small pot. Or you can interpret this metaphorically by planting the seeds of a new habit or attitude in your life. Perhaps it's the habit of regular prayer, journaling, or something fitness related.

Whatever you choose, make a physical note of it on the next page. You can write out your plan, draw a picture, use stickers, or take a picture.

It's not enough to decide in our minds. If we don't record our plan somewhere, we have a much greater likelihood of failing to follow through.

MY SEEDLING IS:

A Prayer

About Leaving Failure Behind

"Don't rejoice against me, my enemy.
When I fall, I will arise. When I sit in
darkness, Yahweh will be a light to me"
(Micah 7:8 WEB).

Dear Lord, I need help changing the focus of my thoughts and my words about myself. During this difficult time I've let so many responsibilities and projects fall to the wayside. And a lot of what I have done has been only mediocre quality. I'm so far behind; it feels like I'll never catch up.

Am I really this much of a failure? I can't recall anything I've done well in such a long time. And now the question I'm most afraid to ask. Have I disappointed You?

I know a lot of my negative thoughts about myself aren't true. But once a thought begins they *all* swarm in my head, and I don't know how to banish them. Lead me to the Scripture that shows I'm not beyond hope. Put people in my life who have been where I am. Don't leave me in this desolate place.

Yet even as I pray, I can feel Your Spirit whispering words of love to me. I can begin to see the difference between the whispered lies and the light of truth. Help me build on this and remember Your great love for me. You made the ultimate sacrifice for me so I could walk closely with You. Remind me that You care deeply about me, not what I can accomplish.

You are an amazing God. Listening to the tiniest whimper of pain from Your children. You hide us in Your strong tower, You fight for us, and You continually bless us. We deserve nothing, but Your great love knows no bounds. Thank You for Your sustaining strength in times of trouble. Amen.

3 Scripture Prescriptions to Meet God Where You Are

Few of us wouldn't go see a doctor when we're ill. But for some reason, when our souls are ailing, we often avoid seeking out the recommendations of our heavenly physician. This list of Bible verses is what I like to term, Scripture Prescriptions.

I recommend you decorate the verses and write what God is saying to you through each of them.

I also urge you to copy them onto index cards and tape them around your home and car. The constant reminder that God has an answer to what is wrong can bring us the peace we're so desperately craving.

"Give all your worries and cares to God, for
he cares about you"
(Peter 5:7 NLT).

"And He said to them, 'Come away by
yourselves to a secluded place and
rest a while.' (For there were many
people coming and going, and they
did not even have time to eat)"
(Mark 6:31 NASB).

"The Lord replied, 'My Presence will go
with you, and I will give you rest'"
(Exodus 33:14 NIV).

Chapter Two—*Rediscovering Peace*

Rediscovering God's peace—no matter what circumstances we face—must be the place we start when we're searching for relief from weariness. As we saw in the previous chapter, there are many obstacles to finding—and dwelling—in that peace. But once we've identified them, we can move forward.

I used to think that peace was the absence of strife. But thankfully that's a shallow, and not very helpful, worldly definition. Instead, when we dive deep into God's Word searching for examples of His peace, we find that it comes during—and despite—difficult circumstances.

That's the peace we're promised, and that's the peace we're going to reclaim.

A Devotion

To Remind Me God's Love Isn't Performance Based

"The Lord will fight for you, and you shall hold your peace" (Exodus 14:14 NKJV).

Many years ago I was in a meeting and several people were telling one of my co-workers what she should do. She listened quietly for a time, but as the burden of what they thought she needed to do became too much to bear, she held up her hands. "Stop." She stood to her feet, keeping her voice firm, but pleasant, "Please don't *should* on me."

For a moment everyone stared at her.

Then our boss began to chuckle. After we'd all expressed our admiration of her handling of a difficult situation, we began to work together to find solutions that didn't lay the entire mess on her.

Don't *should* on me.

It's a phrase that has come to my mind for many reasons and different occasions. Sometimes the imposed *shoulds* come from others. Sometimes they originate in my mind.

I'm good at thinking up what I *should* do, especially when I'm faced with life's challenges. I often think I must make certain progress or attempt specific actions before going to God for help. But that perception isn't at all accurate. God doesn't give me a to-do list that I must finish before I receive His help. Instead, He comes alongside me, right where I am without chastising me about how I got there. He returns my peace—and dispels my weariness— by fighting the battles I cannot and walking with me through situations I cannot face alone.

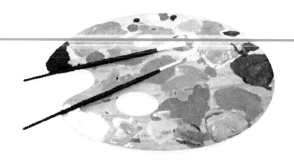

Forging A Creative Connection

Letting go of the *shoulds* can be a challenge. *Shoulds* feel like they belong. So today we're going to begin to collect all the *shoulds* that we can think of. Nothing is off limits. You are master of this operation.

Let's make a list, but because some parts of my *should* list are private, I want you to get or make an envelope. Decorate it and then tape it on the next page. Then write out your shoulds—each on a different piece of paper. Alternatively you could type your *should*, print it out, and cut the words apart.

Stuff the envelope with the words and phrases you've come up with. And leave them in there. Don't ever let them stick to you again.

A Prayer

To Help Me Let Go of Expectations

"We are hard pressed on every side, but not crushed; perplexed, but not in despair; persecuted, but not abandoned; struck down, but not destroyed" (2 Corinthians 4:8-9 NIV).

Dear Lord, life is pushing in on me. The weight of it is a burden and has become so much more than I can bear. Everywhere I turn I meet with the expectations of what I should have done and tasks that still need doing. Help me out of this place.

Show me the steps I can take and lead me to release the others. Give me Your eyes and Your mind to set my priorities. Too much needs my attention. How do I prioritize it all into any kind of a logical fashion?

Remind me that You have a plan and purpose, and that my ineptness won't interfere. Let me see You at work to jumpstart my peace as I begin to pull back from my to-do list and lean into Your strength.

You are my rock, my fortress, and the place I run for comfort and peace. Don't ever let me forget You again, no matter what chaos surrounds me. Amen.

A Devotion

To Remind Me That God's Perspective Brings Peace and Rest

"Open my eyes so that I may contemplate wonderful things from Your instruction" (Psalm 119:18 HCSB).

Where I look matters.

That statement is basic—and obvious. I overlooked its importance. My husband and I love to go to the Blue Ridge mountains for a day away. We often go to hike or drive the Blue Ridge Parkway, and I always have my camera with me. The time in God's creation helps us reconnect with God, and with each other.

One afternoon, as we were enjoying the view from the top of Mount Mitchell, my husband spied a hawk. I immediately brought up my camera and tried to spot the bird through the viewfinder. I searched and searched through that tiny lens, unable to find what I was looking for. The more I tried, the more frustrated I got. As I voiced my irritation at not being able to see the bird, I felt my husband's hands on my shoulders, gently turning me toward the place where the bird dipped and dived. I had been looking in the wrong direction.

After I got home and looked at my pictures, I was struck by the spiritual application of my experience. I had some great pictures of the bird, but only because my husband had guided me where to look.

God guides us like that. Without His direction, we can't see what we're looking for. But when we let Him guide us, the answers we're looking for become clear.

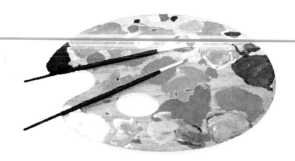

Forging a Creative Connection

Today we're going to practice looking from a different perspective. I'm going to give you several ideas of how you can do this, but don't limit yourself to my suggestions. If something else seems to fit, go for it. There is a place for you to write about your experience on the next page.

Different Perspectives

1. Go outside. Sit on the ground. Choose one tiny object—a blade of grass, wildflower, insect, or speck of gravel. Study it. Look for colors. Notice how the object fits in

relation to its immediate surroundings. Record your observations and ask God how He would like to speak to you through this exercise.

2. Go into your dining room or kitchen. Sit in a different chair than where you normally sit and observe at how your perspective has changed. What can you see that you couldn't before? What can't you see? For extra credit, talk your family into everyone changing where they sit and discuss the differences.

3. Drive a familiar road. Choose a parking lot where you've never stopped before and turn in. Sit in your car and watch the traffic go by. What do you see differently from this perspective? Record your observations and ask God how He would like to speak to you through this exercise.

4. Go outside. Choose a place where there are trees above you. Now look straight up. Notice the patterns against the sky. It doesn't matter if it's day or night, use a few minutes to see what's above you. Record your observations and ask God how He would like to speak to you through this exercise.

Record Your Observations:

What did you see?

How did your perspective change?

How did God speak to you through this exercise?

If He brought any Bible verses to mind, record them here.

A Prayer

Asking You to Give Me Your Eyes to See This Situation

"'For my thoughts are not your thoughts, neither are your ways my ways,' declares the Lord. 'As the heavens are higher than the earth, so are my ways higher than your ways and my thoughts than your thoughts'" (Isaiah 55:8-9 NIV).

Dear Lord, I'm battling weariness right now. It's not only that my mind and body are exhausted, but I'm sick and tired of this situation. I want the circumstances to change, but I have no way to make that happen.

Your Holy Word promises that You will make all work together for good. Can I have a preview of how that applies in this circumstance? My eyes are dry because of all the tears I've shed, but I can't see any hope. I want to be faithful, but this time hope seems so difficult.

I know You still work miracles. I need one right now. Please turn me in the right direction for this struggle. Guide my steps and my thoughts. You love me and I believe You do. Remind me of all the times You've led me to victory. Replace my weariness with strength. Change me, change my attitude, and then use me to make a difference in the lives of those around me. Amen.

A Devotion

About Becoming a Stone Dropper

"When they persisted in questioning Him,
He stood up and said to them, 'The one
without sin among you should be the first
to throw a stone at her'" (John 8:7 HCSB).

Imagine with me the scene that day. A woman has been caught in the act of adultery. In biblical times, it's a crime punishable by death—death by stoning. The men and women drag her into the public square. I can hear the voices of her accusers, raised in hatred and condemnation.

"You're nothing but filth."

"You knew what could happen when you made your choice."

"Get rid of her. We can't have someone like her contaminating our town."

She's thrown at the feet of a famous teacher, for Him to pronounce the death sentence. Why did they bring her to Him? Because He's known for His compassion. By bringing her crime to His attention they could accomplish two goals. They can get rid of a sinner and either expose Him as a liar, or a lawbreaker.

Instead, Jesus introduces them all to the concept of grace.

And He does it without compromising the law or the heart of compassion He's known for.

Back in the viewpoint of our sinner, I can imagine her laying there at His feet, covering her head with her arms as she tries to make as small a target as possible. Every muscle is tensed, waiting for the first stone from the angry mob.

As the crowd begins to quiet, instead of the sound of stones whistling through the air, she hears the words of the teacher. His pronouncement takes them all by surprise—even her. And I can imagine that the next sounds she hears are the thumps all around her as the stones drop to the ground.

The obvious lesson we learn from this event is to extend grace to others. But equally as important, we must extend grace to ourselves. When weariness crowds in, the failures also tend to overwhelm us. The overwhelmed times are when we need to stop throwing stones at ourselves. I've learned to make a conscious effort to drop those stones and be an instrument of grace—even to myself.

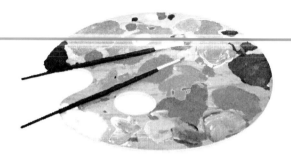

Forging A Creative Connection

This creative connection is going to require at least two rocks, and a permanent marker or paint. If you can't find a stone, cut some pieces of paper into stone shapes.

On your rock, write an accusation made against you. It can be a complaint you've made against yourself or an accusation someone else has made again you. When you're done, either go outside and throw the stone as far away from you as possible, or bury it in the ground. Doing this symbolizes that Jesus has covered the accusation with love.

Now use the second rock to record a promise, or a word, or a thought that God gave you to replace the accusation. Keep that rock somewhere you can see it daily.

A Prayer

To Keep Me From Throwing Stones at Myself

"If we confess our sins, he is faithful and just and will forgive us our sins and purify us from all unrighteousness" (1 John 1:9 NIV).

Dear Lord, I've failed in so many areas of my life, and they're all coming to light right now. I can't bear to look in a mirror because all I see is defeat. There's so much to do that it's impossible to do everything. I go from task to task and only get further behind. Your perspective is what I need.

Everywhere I turn I see only condemnation. I know I haven't done as I should, but surely I'm not as much of a failure as they say. Please help me quiet the voices inside and out. Send people to me to encourage me.

Show me how to replace the accusations with Your truth. I want Your truth. Help me see the mistakes I've made so I don't make them again. But along with that, let me see the areas where I've done well. Release me from any false guilt I'm carrying, and don't let me get tangled in it again.

Most of all, help me learn from this experience. Don't let me be the voice of accusation in someone else's life. Instead, remind me to encourage those I meet, even when they've messed up. Speak Your love to others through me, even as You've whispered encouragement and grace to me. Amen.

A Devotion

About Being, Not Doing

"You do not want a sacrifice, or I would give it; You are not pleased with a burnt offering" (Psalm 51:16 HCSB).

I don't know about you, but I'm a doer. No matter how hard I try, I can't seem to help myself. And while I have made some improvement over the years, unless I'm really focused, I'm will judge my day, my progress, even my worth, on my accomplishments.

I know in my head that a check mark by everything on my to-do list isn't synonymous for

81

how well I'm doing. Unfortunately, I can't seem to get my feelings to switch over to this way of thinking. This unhealthy outlook permeates every part of my life, especially spiritually. I keep acting like I can win God's favor by doing more.

It's time to refocus my life.

Being a Christ-follower has its emphasis on the state of being verb, rather than an action verb.

God has always been more interested in the process rather than the product.

That sentence reminds me that God is relational, not task, oriented. Whatever needs doing, He can do. He uses us to accomplish His will not to keep us busy or because He Himself doesn't have the time. He allows us to join Him where He's working because of the relationship.

God wants to spend time with me. He wants me to be so familiar with His voice that I can instantly hear and respond when He calls my name. But when I fill my life with activities; my focus drifts, as tasks capture my attention and draw me away from the relationship.

So once again, I'm readjusting my life. I'm looking at the person of God and making concrete plans to spend more time with Him, instead of for Him.

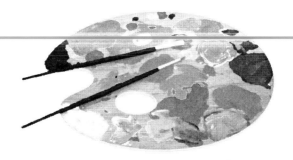

Forging A Creative Connection

Today we're going to get to the heart of the matter. On the next page, I want you to draw several hearts. Inside each one, record the words God uses to describe you. For example: precious, child, beloved, faithful, etc.

Make the hearts as creative or plain as you chose. Embellish each one with colored pens or pencils, stickers, tape, glitter, etc. But I want you to draw at least five different hearts. God wants you to remember how much He loves you. Give Him plenty of room.

A Prayer

About the Trap of Doing

"For the mind-set of the flesh is death, but the mind-set of the Spirit is life and peace" (Romans 8:6 HCSB).

Dear Lord, I've fallen into a familiar trap. Once again, I'm judging my life and my worth by my accomplishments. As life spirals further out of control, my plan-making becomes more desperate. When will I learn that I can't plan myself out of a mess?

Your plans have meaning and order. Every path you set me on has purpose—whether I can see it or not. You have only the best in Your mind for me. Help me remember.

It's only when I'm walking close beside You that I find the peace I so desperately crave. Why do I insist on running ahead? I'm as erratic and unpredictable as a bee flitting from flower to flower.

Recapture my attention. Return my focus to You. Remove the urge to judge myself based on what I've accomplished. Replace it with a sense of peace that comes only from staying in step with You.

You are everything I need, and everything I desire. Flood my soul with a longing to be with You and filter out the urge to *do* instead of be. Amen.

A Devotion

To Remind Me That Words Matter

"Gracious words are a honeycomb, sweet
to the soul and healing to the bones"
(Proverbs 16:24 NIV).

As an author, words have a special place in my heart and in my life. I play with them, study them, and choose them carefully—when I write. But there was a time when I wasn't as careful about the words I spoke, especially to myself.

It had been a difficult few months. I'd been locked in battle after battle. I'd been accused of being prideful, untalented, and even stupid. I was tired of the fight, and I'd begun to believe some of the lies.

After all, these people were only echoing the accusations I've said to myself in the silence of my soul.

I finally took my struggles to God, begging Him to separate the truth from the lies. I was totally honest with Him, admitting what an awful worthless person I was. Instead of agreement, His Spirit sent me to Proverbs 16:24.

His Spirit reminded me that this verse doesn't pertain to only the words I write. He pointed out that I wasn't careful when I chose the words I said to myself.

That's when I recognized that what I said to myself were words I wouldn't allow even the most evil character to say to others. And that negative self-talk had set me up to believe the lies that were being whispered about me and shouted to me. I already believed those falsehoods and now the weight of it was pulling me under.

The truth is, each of us is unique and precious to God. He paid the ultimate price to bring us back to Him.

Yes words matter—even the words we speak to ourselves.

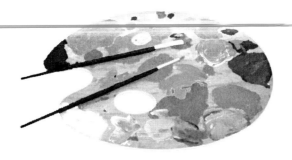

Forging a Creative Connection

Choose one of the words below. Once you've made your choice, think about that word for five minutes. Then write what came to mind. Don't judge positive or negative, just write it all. If your writing brings new ideas, record them as well.

Silent	Margin
Discipline	Future
Remember	Honor
Crown	Serve

Heart   Faith
Light   Create

A Prayer

Asking for Refuge in the Storm

"He made the storm be still, and the waves
of the sea were hushed"
(Psalm 107:29 ESV).

Dear Lord, I'm living life in the middle of a
storm. I'm tired of battling and weary to the bone.
Yet every time I lay my head on the pillow, my

thoughts rage in a maelstrom of their own. Is there no rest anywhere?

I know that I've been trying to manage life all on my own. I don't know why I wait until I'm at a crisis point to call out to You. I've felt Your peace in crazy places, and I know You offer it freely. Help me now.

Start by quieting my thoughts. I need sleep so badly, but my mind won't let me rest. Activities I should have done, need to do, and might forget turn into a tornado that destroys my path to peace. I know You can calm the chaos with a single word. Bring to my mind Bible verses that will soothe and quieten.

I'm asking for a refuge in this storm. My days are so busy, and I need some breathing space somewhere. I don't even know what that kind of beauty could look like. Perhaps a quiet moment between responsibilities. It could be a person to help share the load or a quick phone call from a friend who feels the prompting to pray for me.

Thank You for Your patience with me. I don't feel any condemnation for not turning to You immediately. Help me learn from this and never make this mistake again. Amen.

3 Scripture Prescriptions to Meet God Where You Are

Few of us wouldn't go see a doctor when we're ill. But for some reason, when our souls are ailing, we often avoid seeking out the recommendations of our heavenly physician. This list of Bible verses are what I like to term, Scripture Prescriptions.

I recommend you decorate the verses and write what God is saying to you through each of them.

I also urge you to copy them onto index cards and tape them around your home and car. The constant reminder that God has an answer to what is wrong can bring us the peace we're so desperately craving.

"I have told you all this so that you may have peace in me. Here on earth you will have many trials and sorrows. But take heart, because I have overcome the world"
(John 16:33 NLT).

"You will keep the mind that is dependent on You in perfect peace, for it is trusting in You."
(Isaiah 26:3 HCSB).

"Peace I leave with you; my peace I give to you. Not as the world gives do I give to you. Let not your hearts be troubled, neither let them be afraid"
(John 14:27 ESV).

Chapter Three—*Prayer Play*

Yes, you read the title of this chapter correctly. We're going to explore the play we can find in our prayer time. So often, prayer is treated with solemnity, and even pomp and circumstance. Instead, the heart of prayer is a child spending time with a loving parent.

How sad it would be if the time we spent were with our children was marked by solemn formality? Thankfully it's not. Time with our children and with those we love encompasses the entire range of emotions. Our prayer life needs to reflect those feelings as well.

On the whole, we tend to have the solemn formality part covered. Now it's time to practice the joyful play of prayer. Especially when we're stressed and in crisis we forget the power of prayer play. So we're going to practice this valuable aspect of hanging out with God.

Our interactions with God don't have to be restricted to a certain time and place. Wherever we are and whatever we're doing, He wants to be part of our life. Imagine this chapter as a series of play dates with our Heavenly Father. Oh the fun we're going to have!

A Devotion

To Remind Us That Prayer Play is Another Name for Worship

"Praise Him with tambourine and dance;
praise Him with flute and strings. Praise
Him with resounding cymbals; praise Him
with clashing cymbals. Let everything
that breathes praise the Lord. Hallelujah!"
(Psalm 150:4-6 HCSB).

My prayer life has done a lot of evolving as I've grown and matured spiritually.

As a child, it consisted of two memorized pieces, one said before meals, the other before bed. As I reached my teen years, my friends began to grow in their faith and challenged me to also expand my God-filled horizons. During this time, prayer was something breathed in my mind or whispered in the pages of a diary.

When I got married my husband and I tried to pray together as a couple, but it was hard and awkward. So we stopped and didn't return to the practice again until our kids were grown. However, we did pray with our kids at bedtime and when they were facing difficulties.

It was when I was going through a particularly difficult time that I began to take long walks to talk to God. These weren't conversations in my mind. They were audible—at least on my end—discussions of what my life looked like right then and how I wanted to change. Some days I begged, pleaded, and cried. Other days I sang praises, skipping and almost dancing along because of the ways He was answering my prayers.

That was when I realized prayer could be an active experience.

Not only could it be, but when I prayed this way, it took on a depth and immediacy that I hadn't expected. Now I go out on regular prayer walks.

Sometimes alone, sometimes with others. I often take a camera and/or my cell phone so I can record insights God gives me.

I've learned a valuable lesson about prayer through the years. God is not limited, and neither are the ways we communicate with Him or Him with us.

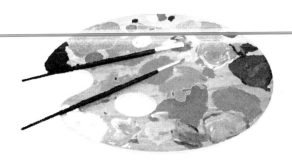

Forging A Creative Connection

With this creative exercise, we're going to take God off the shelf and out of the box. I want you to take a walk and talk to God—out loud. You can choose someplace off the beaten path, walk around your neighborhood, or through a parking lot. The idea is to get away and start an actual conversation with your Heavenly Father.

When you return, come back here and record some of what you said and what you felt like God had to say in return. I want you to do this every day for five days, making notes each day.

Finally I want you to sum up the exercise and note any changes in the conversation as they days went by.

Day 1

Day 2

Day 3

Day 4

Day 5

What changes did you see over the five days? How will you continue your daily conversations with God? Record your thoughts below.

A Prayer

Asking God to Bring the Joy of Prayer

"The Lord your God in your midst, The Mighty One, will save; He will rejoice over you with gladness, He will quiet you with His love, He will rejoice over you with singing" (Zephaniah 3:17 NKJV).

Dear Lord, please forgive me. I've put You in a prayer box and set You on the shelf. I only take You down on formal occasions or when I'm facing desperate circumstances. Today I want that all to change.

I've tried a lot of different ways to pray and read books on the subject. But I have to confess that our time together feels awkward and stiff. Show me how to interact with You in a different way.

I don't want our time together to always be serious business, but in some ways that idea seems disrespectful. Show me how to be joyful with You.

You are my Heavenly Father, and I want to spend time with You. Will You show me how? Don't let me be shy or nervous about what I should say. Instead remind me that You chose me as I was. No amount of cleaning up could make You love me more.

Renew our time together in unexpected ways and in unexpected places. I want to share more of my time with You. Lead me into a deeper—more joyful—relationship with You. Amen.

A Devotion

About The Healing Power of Praise

"But you are holy, you who inhabit the praises of Israel" (Psalm 22:3 WEB).

It had been a brutal few days. My father's battle with Alzheimer's was coming to an end. While it was good that he wouldn't be suffering much longer, we were all beyond exhausted. We'd huddled by his bedside, only occasionally slipping out for a quick bite to eat. At lunch that day, my husband insisted I get further away than the cafeteria, so I walked toward my car and drove to a drive-through restaurant

My eyes were gritty and dry. Driving was almost too much effort, but no matter how I tried, I couldn't seem to overcome the utter weariness that invaded my soul. Then I turned on the car radio.

My favorite praise song came streaming through the speakers, and I felt my spirits lift. The day was warm so I rolled down the windows and opened the sunroof, letting the sun invade the car. The music continued, and I began to sing along.

With each familiar note, more of the burden slipped away. The music ended and another familiar tune began. Song after song, God used the music on the radio to renew my spirit and heal me from the exhaustion.

By the time I'd eaten and returned to the assisted care facility where my father lay, I was strong and refreshed.

That hasn't been the only time that singing praise to God has healed my spirit. It's happened again and again. Now, when I'm battling stress and weariness, praise music is the first place I turn.

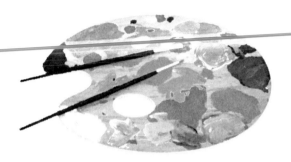

Forging A Creative Connection

Today we're going to begin a gratitude journal. This exercise is going to take a month to complete. I want you to draw a grid with 7 columns and 5 rows. This will give you 35 boxes. In the upper right hand corner of each box write a number—**1** thru **30** (yes you'll have some boxes left over). Each day, write one phrase of gratitude. Do you best not to repeat anything. Look for new blessings each day. It doesn't matter if your numbers match the actual dates. The point is to do this activity for a month.

A Prayer

To Release The Power of Thanksgiving

"Whatever you do in word or deed, do
all in the name of the Lord Jesus, giving
thanks through Him to God the Father"
(Colossians 3:17 NASB).

Dear Lord, You are the Creator of everything.
Your work is limitless and Your majesty knows no
bounds. All of creation testifies to Your greatness.

111

Yet, You care about me. I was created in Your image, Your breath fills my soul. I could begin to tell of all the ways You've blessed me and the list would never come to an end.

Even the discipline you administer is worthy of praise. There is never any condemnation, only correction and reconciliation. Teach me to be more like You. Empty me of myself, and fill me with You.

As I go through my days, don't let me neglect to see Your hand in everything around me. Make me pause as I'm once again filled with wonder at Your amazing love. Make the weariness I battle fall away as I refocus on Your provision.

Remind me of Your constant presence. Don't let my situation blot out the fact of Your presence. You are worthy to be praised, let me always make praise a priority in my life. Amen.

A Devotion

To Remind Us the Importance of Recording What Happened

"The Lord answered me: Write down this vision; clearly inscribe it on tablets so one may easily read it" (Habakkuk 2:2 HCSB).

I used to apply this verse to my life in the context of my public writing. I took it as confirmation that my words were for others to read. Now I've discovered that like so much of God's Word, this verse has a much wider application.

One evening I collapsed into bed, too tired to sleep, but unable to concentrate on reading a book—not even the Bible. So I reached for my journal, intending to record my thoughts and make some sense out of the chaos that had so exhausted me. The journal was almost full, and I had to search to find a blank page. As I searched for space to write, my words drew me in. That's when God began to speak.

The pages held fairly recent memories, yet I'd already forgotten many of the details of what God had done. Reading about the way God had worked was a revelation. Those recent memories prompted me to pull out some older journals, and soon I was deep into the written record of God's faithfulness throughout my life.

As I read I could feel the vise-like grip of stress, along with the malaise of weariness ease. Over and over I had recorded where and how God had answered my prayers. In my hands I held the proof of His faithfulness. The act of reading about it made the memories come alive. As I read about God's provision, I experienced it all over again.

That experience gave me one more reason to keep up my journaling ways. I was recording His faithfulness, not necessarily for the world, but for me.

Forging A Creative Connection

Instead of tablets, we're going to use some leaves to help us record what God has spoken. Either go outside and gather some leaves or cut some leaf shapes from paper. On each leaf, record a word or two that brings to mind an answered prayer. The prayer could have been one you prayed for yourself or on behalf of someone else.

Now tape those leaves into this book. You can decorate the page further, or leave it plain. The idea is to get used to taking note of times when God answers our prayers.

A Prayer

Asking That I Never Forget

"My soul, praise the Lord, and do not
forget all His benefits"
(Psalm 103:2 HCSB).

Dear Lord, Your faithfulness to me knows no
bounds. Through the years You've answered more

prayers than I can remember—many of the answers coming before I asked.

I've tried to write down what You've said and done, but there's so much I didn't record. But You never forget. You can bring to my mind how You've worked before.

I want to remember all the ways You've been there for me, especially now. I feel so overwhelmed and weary. With that exhaustion comes hopelessness. Don't let me give in and give up.

Instead, renew my strength by replaying memories of how You've always been by my side. Even when I wasn't aware of Your presence You were always there. I've never been abandoned or alone.

It didn't matter if the obstacle I faced was massive or tiny, You were still there with us. It was Your strength that sustained me, Your breath that gave me hope, and Your words of love whispered into my soul when I was past my abilities.

You've taken care of me, and I've witnessed You at work in the lives of those around me. Don't let me forget the miracles You've worked in their lives. Don't ever let any of us forget You are always with us. Amen.

A Devotion

About The Master Artist

"In the beginning God created"
(Genesis 1:1 NLT).

My mother is an artist, and I've always admired the sure strokes she uses as she applies color to canvas. The pictures she's created aren't dictated by the tools she uses or her circumstances. Her paintings are controlled by the vision she holds so firmly in her mind.

In her mind's eye, the picture was always finished before she began. But to me, watching it take shape often looked more like chaos than art.

In our lives, God is the artist. And even if what is happening right now looks like chaos, we can be certain that He has the end result in mind. The colors He uses to paint our lives may not be the blues and greens an artist uses. Instead, the colors He uses are experiences, emotions, and people. They infuse our lives with vibrancy.

He wields His soft brush with masterful strokes, allowing enough shadow and darkness to bring out the brilliance of the light. From up close, the colors may look muddy and the shapes indistinct, but viewed from a distance, each life is a masterpiece.

So whether our lives are being covered in drab colors of grey and brown, or highlighted by vibrant yellows and reds, we can rest assured the end product will be beautiful.

Forging A Creative Connection

Think about a specific time when God answered a prayer. It doesn't have to be a big prayer, just one that you remember. Write everything you can remember about that situation. Who was involved, why it was important, and any Bible verse associated with that experience. Decorate the page. Draw, color, and add stickers or tape.

An answered Prayer

A Prayer

About The Beauty in My Life

"Finally, brothers and sisters, whatever is true, whatever is noble, whatever is right, whatever is pure, whatever is lovely, whatever is admirable—if anything is excellent or praiseworthy—think about such things" (Philippians 4:8 NIV).

Dear Lord, I've become so focused on being weary I no longer noticed the beauty surrounding me. I've allowed a filter of fatigue and weariness to reduce my life to nothing but drab black and white. You've given the world around me color and beauty, and I've been oblivious to it for far too long.

Help me to experience life in living color once again. You have blessed me with rich tapestry of friends and family. I've been so tired that all I've been focusing on is the tangled threads instead of the beautiful picture. Remind me to appreciate those who've been supporting me through this difficult time.

Give me new eyes to see the good in my life. I'm ready to once again look up and see all the loveliness I know is there. You are faithful, and I know You love me in ways I cannot begin to imagine. Show me the miracles of a life lived with You. Don't let me get so bogged down that I forget to praise You.

Replace the black and white negative with the full color version of my life. When I begin to get pulled under, bring Your promises and Your answered prayers to my mind. Change my habits and let me once again enjoy the beauty of walking with You. Amen.

A Devotion

About A Single Drop of Water

"For this is what the Lord God says: See, I Myself will search for My flock and look for them" (Ezekiel 34:11 HCSB).

Photography is my second love and is a passion almost as consuming as committing words to paper. It's not unusual for me to spend hours at a time wandering through the beautiful scenery near where we live. Frequently my husband is with me, patiently waiting as I explore God's creation through the lens of my camera.

One day, a glistening drop of water caught my eye. As I investigated, I found that the foliage on a plant growing next to the river collected the spray from a nearby waterfall. As the leaves drooped from the weight, the water dripped from the tip of the leaves. The sun highlighted each drop as it formed, grew heavy, and dropped into the rushing water.

Driven to capture this beautiful sight with my lens, I contorted myself and my camera into a precarious position. My husband stood to one side shaking his head. "Only you would chase after a single drop of water when there's a roaring waterfall in front of you."

After I got home, his words continued to echo in my head as I felt the Spirit nudge me toward a revelation. Sometimes life is like a rushing river or waterfall. It's hard to keep up or even hear anything over the noise of life. But God sees each of us like that drop of water. We're never part of the crowd. To Him, we're each precious and beautiful.

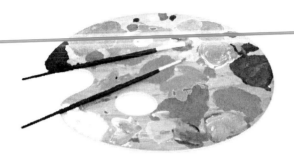

Forging a Creative Connection

I want you to study an object near you. Then I want you to draw it below. The focus of this exercise is to hone our powers of observation, not stress ourselves out because we're not master artists. But the fact is that God has surrounded us by beauty and we need to get in the habit of seeing that beauty.

A Prayer
About Prayer

"In the same way the Spirit also helps our weakness; for we do not know how to pray as we should, but the Spirit Himself intercedes for us with groanings too deep for words" (Romans 8:26 NASB).

Dear Lord, my prayer life has drained away to almost nothing. More often than not I seem to run away from talking to You. I've let the weariness of this season drag me down and put up a barrier between us. Now I can see that my lack of time spent with You is affecting my days and nights.

Help me change this pattern and go back to the way it used to be. I want You to be the first person I run to—whether I'm tired, joyful, or going about my normal day. I miss my routine of spending time with You every morning, and whispering good night as I lay my head on my pillow each evening.

I'm ashamed that I've moved away from time with You, and I've let that shame drive me even further away. Break that cycle and help me overcome my fear. Don't let me falter as I come back. Keep my busy schedule and my exhaustion from being an excuse I use not to meet with You.

Clear my schedule and use Your Spirit to remind me to come to You first. Banish my feelings of fear and condemnation. I know that in You, there is no condemnation. Welcome Your wayward child back with loving arms and the covering of peace that I remember so well. Amen.

3 Scripture Prescriptions to Meet God Where You Are

There are very few of us who wouldn't go see a doctor when we're ill. But for some reason, when our souls are ailing, we often avoid seeking out the recommendations of our heavenly physician. This list of Bible verses are what I like to term, Scripture prescriptions.

I recommend you decorate the verses and write what God is saying to you through each of them.

I also urge you to copy them onto index cards and tape them around your home and car. The constant reminder that God has an answer to what is wrong can bring us the peace we're so desperately craving.

"Speaking to one another in psalms and hymns and spiritual songs, singing and making melody with your heart to the Lord" (Ephesians 5:19 NASB).

"Rejoice in our confident hope. Be patient in trouble, and keep on praying" (Romans 12:12 NLT).

"Through Jesus, therefore, let us continually offer to God a sacrifice of praise—the fruit of lips that openly profess his name" (Hebrews 13:15 NIV).

Chapter Four—*Letting Go*

Letting go and giving your mind and body time to rest is essential during any season of crisis. It's also one of the hardest things to do. To understand what it means to rest we must endure a short English lesson about verbs. In modern English, a verb signifies the action or state of being of the subject. Verbs are either active or passive, they either let their subjects perform an action or receive an action.

Why is this important? Because as a believer, my primary purpose can be found in a state of being verb. I rest in God and allow Him to do His work through me. He's the one doing the heavy lifting, not me.

Many of us make the mistake of reading the Bible and seeing it as a list of commands. There are instances when we are commanded to take action, but most of the time that isn't actually the case. It would be more accurate to look at the Bible as a list of what to-be instead of a list of what to-do. So much of what we take to be orders to do something are orders to be something so that God can do the work through us.

How does that help us when we already have too much to do and not enough hours in the day? It gives us permission to let go—activities, actions, and events that were never ours to do in the first place. Learning how to let go is a process. And this is the chapter where we will begin clearing out those unnecessary to-dos.

A Devotion

About Developing the Habit of Rest

"In vain you rise early and stay up late, toiling for food to eat—for he grants sleep to those he loves" (Psalm 127:2 NIV).

When I was in the midst of developing a fitness routine for the first time, there was a steep learning curve. I had to figure out where in my schedule a regular—daily—workout time would fit. I had to find a gym where I felt most comfortable, and I had to learn to operate all the machines.

Learning how to use the machines may seem like the easiest to do, but it was the one that stressed me out the most. I think if I'd been doing it somewhere private, it wouldn't have been so bad. But I was in a public place and there were frequently others waiting on me to finish so they could have a turn.

While I was learning how to manage the strength training portion of my workout routine, my instructor emphasized the importance of letting my muscles rest between sets. I heard what was said, but putting that admonition into practice was more difficult. Sitting still without using a machine for a full minute was tough—especially when others were waiting. So I pretty much ignored that portion of the training.

It turns out that by skipping the rest periods, I wasn't allowing my muscles to recover, and this lack of rest affected the muscle-building I was trying to do. Our muscles need that short one to two minute time to recover and this rest time help build stronger muscles. It also prevents muscle damage.

You know where I'm going with this, right? Our lives are the same way. We cannot keep working without a rest. God has designed us—physically, spiritually, and emotionally—for a healthy rhythm of work and rest. When these get out of balance, our strength suffers. Resting may often seem like a frivolous pursuit, but in truth it's the best thing we can do to stay strong—for ourselves and for those around us.

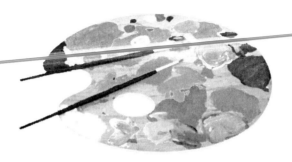

Forging A Creative Connection

I want you to set a timer or an alarm clock for five minutes. Turn off all external noise, such as television or radio. Close your eyes and listen. Try not to let your mind wander or make to-do lists. Instead listen to the sounds and silences around you.

When the five minutes is up, record what you experienced. You can write about what you heard or draw pictures. Make sure you also record anything God might have said or any insight you gained through the exercise.

A Prayer

Asking God to Teach Me the Rhythm of Rest

"Then Jesus said to them, "The Sabbath was made to meet the needs of people, and not people to meet the requirements of the Sabbath" (Mark 2:27 NLT).

Dear Lord, I am once again in a crisis. My weariness is affecting me, but when I try to rest, I feel guilty. Is this a normal season when rest isn't possible? Could I have been deceived into thinking rest should be a priority in my life? Help me know how to stop this vicious circle.

I know I've read about the importance of a Sabbath rest in the Bible, but I don't know how to make that happen in my life. Taking an entire day without work seems frivolous in the extreme. I can't seem to lay down my phone because others are counting on me, much less find an hour to slip away. How have I come to this point, and how do I reverse course and end up somewhere else?

Show me what it looks like to rest when life is spiraling out of control. Calm my anxious thoughts and lead me into peaceful paths. I don't know how long I can continue at this pace.

My priorities are driven by what's most urgent, instead of governed by Your instruction. Show me how to make the changes needed.

Put others into my life who've dealt with times like this. Open my eyes to hear what they have to say. Don't let me continue on this path. Redirect my steps onto the road You have for me. Only You can provide the peace I so desperately need. Make the changes necessary to bring me back to Your side and out of the chaos I'm facing now. Amen.

A Devotion

To Remind Me that It's God's Work, Not Mine That Matters

"For it is God who works in you to will and to act in order to fulfill his good purpose" (Philippians 2:13 NIV).

A few years ago I had the opportunity to visit Ethiopia on a mission trip. It was a life-changing experience, and the lessons I learned there have been refined after coming home.

During that trip, I realized my inability to make a small dent in the needs I saw on every side.

Everywhere I turned, every second of the day, I was surrounded by people with needs. I'd only been in the country for a few hours when I realized how powerless I was to meet these needs. I knew immediately that the only way I'd be of any use at all was if God chose to use me—and He could only use me if I was focused on Him.

In this unfamiliar place, I was forced to let Him set my priorities. His Spirit guided me to those I gave money to, those I shared the love of God with, even when and where I went. And once I leaned in close and let Him work through me, directing my steps, I saw some amazing results.

After coming home, I've realized how much mental and physical energy I waste on trying to manage my life. There are times when I work nonstop trying to fulfill my needs and the needs of those close to me. Without God's guidance, it's an exhausting—and ineffective—endeavor. The only time I'm able to offer help in a situation is when I allow God to do His work through me.

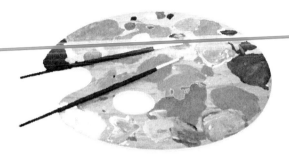

Forging A Creative Connection

We're going to stretch our faith wings today. I want you to cut seven 1 by 3 inch slips of paper. On one side of each one, write a different Bible verse and either a short prayer or the words, "Someone is praying for you today."

Fold each piece of paper in half length-wise and write, "A note for you" on the outside. Now take them with you and when you're out, leave them in places where someone can find them. For the next week, remember to pray for the person who picked up each note. Also ask God to give you a glimpse at how He is using your notes.

In addition, record the verses and prayers in the section below. Embellish the page any way you like.

7 Bible Verses

A Prayer

Asking God to Help Me Get Out of His Way

"Can all your worries add a single moment
to your life? And if worry can't accomplish
a little thing like that, what's the use of
worrying over bigger things?"
(Luke 12:25-26 NLT).

Dear Lord, I need You to take over the management of my life. I'm not doing so well right now. I'm exhausted and weary beyond words. I know it's because I've gone off on my way and left You far behind. I've tried to solve problems without consulting You first. I've taken on too much alone.

You are my strength and salvation. How could I have forgotten? I know that these circumstances aren't my fault. But the way I've tried to handle them without You is my doing. I didn't actually sit down and decide everything would be better if I didn't consult You. I got so caught up in the busyness that I didn't stop to think.

My Bible reading dropped to the wayside because, first I was too busy, then I was too tired. Next I began to neglect my prayer life and before I knew it, I'd ended up in this wasteland of exhaustion and confusion.

Please forgive me. Rescue me from my circumstances and from myself. Then impress the lessons I'm learning about straying from Your side deeply into my mind and heart. Don't ever let me move this far from You again. Hold me close and give me the rest that I can only find when I'm walking close by Your side. Amen.

About Letting Go in the Midst of Weariness

"I have said these things to you, that in
me you may have peace. In the world you
will have tribulation. But take heart; I have
overcome the world"
(Philippians 4:7 HCSB).

When we're in the midst of a season of
weariness, it's seldom an option to quit participating
in life. We have responsibilities, commitments, and
others depending on us. I've found that the key to

combatting weariness in that situation is to find a way to shift my burdens to God.

He promises us peace, no matter the circumstances, and during one difficult season in my life, I decided to take Him up on His offer.

Life swirled around me, pulling in every direction and leaving me no room to recover. My father was at the end of his battle with Alzheimer's; I had a book due; and I was scheduled to speak at back-to-back events. On top of everything else, I came down with a bad case of the flu.

Instead of easing the situation, the forced rest increased the stress. On top of all my commitments, I was stuck in bed, more worried and anxious than ever and unable to do a single thing about what was happening.

In my specific circumstances, I couldn't stop caring for my father, default on my book contract, or cancel speaking engagements. Yet God's Word had to still be true. He promised me peace. How could I find it right there and right then?

That's when God showed up and taught me what letting go of burdens looked like in real time.

He helped me see that the bulk of my weariness stemmed from the mental acceptance of the responsibility of the outcome. It was the responsibility I'd hijacked—and that, much more than the physical actions—was dragging me so far down.

God's part in our lives is making all things work together for good. Our part is to open ourselves up to His strength, and let Him work through us. Then we leave the responsibility of the ultimate outcome to Him. By doing our best—whatever that looks like in the moment—and offering it to Him, we shift the burden to His capable hands.

We see the example of this again and again in the life of Jesus. He did what He was physically able to do, then left the results to God. He didn't drive Himself past exhaustion because He listened to God's priorities and kept them. I believe it was this mindset that allowed Him the wisdom to walk away from the crowds and into time with the Father.

There's no better example to follow than His.

As I waded through the difficult time, I kept my eyes firmly fixed on God. I kept up with my morning devotion time—sometimes listening to the Bible in the car and praying on the way to the facility where my father was being cared for. And I did the next thing, no matter how inadequate it seemed.

I put in the time it took to write the book. Again and again I sat at the computer empty, yet God never failed me. Ideas flowed through my fingers onto the screen. It didn't feel like my best work at the time, but God took my pitiful offering and made it beautiful. I had to cancel one of my speaking engagements because of the illness, but someone was right there able to fill in, and I learned later the event was greatly blessed by her presence. Yes, there were things that were left undone by me, but none of God's plans suffered. He is able—even when we're not.

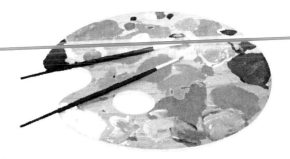

Forging A Creative Connection

It's time to make a list. I want you to think of all the responsibilities you put on yourself, when those responsibilities are God's. Under each responsibility, write what you can and cannot do in regard to that task. Here's an example:

Keep my kids safe

I can set healthy boundaries and teach them about safety, but ultimately it's God who watches over them, especially when I'm not with them.

My List of Incorrectly Assumed Responsibilities:

A Prayer

Asking God to Show Me What it Means to Dwell

"The Lord is my rock, my fortress, and my savior; my God is my rock, in whom I find protection. He is my shield, the power that saves me, and my place of safety"
(Psalm 18:2 NLT).

Dear Lord, I feel like I'm living twenty-four-hour-days in the middle of Grand Central Station.

There's no longer any rhythm to my life. It's nothing but an all-out effort, and the constant drain is taking its toll on my life and on the lives of those near me.

All I want to do is find some place to hide. I crave the peacefulness of solitude. But more than quiet in my environment, I want to find a way to quiet my mind.

Will You show me what it means to dwell with You, and let You dwell with me? Surely the peace found in Your presence can be mine. I know it's available. I've read about it in Your Holy Word.

It's so easy for me to move from Your side and once again end up in the midst of chaos and strife. Show me how to navigate my daily life while sticking close to Your side. Bring people into my life who have learned this lesson and let me learn from them.

I want to be swept beneath Your wings and curl up close. When I'm with You, my perspective changes. The concerns that drive me from rest melt away. Dwelling with You keeps worry far away. Keep me close by Your side and never let me leave. Amen.

A Devotion

About The Myth of Doing it All

"I can do all things through Christ who strengthens me" (Philippians 4:13 NKJV).

This was one of the first Bible verses I ever memorized. It's a heady verse for someone like me. Someone who loves to say yes for two reasons— the sheer joy of being involved and the fear others wouldn't like me if I couldn't perform. It is a dangerous combination. But I thought this verse gave me the ability to say yes to everything, and God would provide a way.

Fast forward several years, and the price of saying yes began to take its toll on my mind and body. I no longer lived a life of joy and victory. Instead I was a slave to over-commitment. And I finally broke. It wasn't pretty. Diagnosed with severe depression and several other mental health challenges, it took me months to recover.

It was a painful lesson and one I had to learn to be able to move forward. When forced to give up everything, I thought I'd never get to do anything fun again and that everyone would dislike me. (*Stupid I know, but it's really what I believed.*) Slowly I began to realize God's plan didn't involve me saying yes to every good activity or need within my community.

I also discovered that when I said yes to something that wasn't intended for me, I was in the way. I'd taken a task from someone else and denied them the joy of obedience. I'd become a roadblock in the journey God had for them.

I've also learned not to equate a need with a call from God. *Because I see a hole that needs filling, it's not my job to jump in.* God has proven perfectly capable of providing for the needs of those around me.

Now I'm living a much more balanced and joyful life. I'm still not perfect. There are days I still can't say no. When I pick up a job or a burden on my own, no matter how small the time commitment, it weighs on me like a ton of bricks. That in itself makes me wary about saying yes without hearing from God.

To sum it all up.

I've learned that I really can do it all...as long as I'm not trying to do everything at once.

Today I encourage you to look at the balance in your life. Do you need to lay something down that's intended for someone else? Are you crying out for rest because you're carrying a load not meant for you? There is rest and peace; all you have to do is let go.

Forging A Creative Connection

In the space, draw a rough floor plan of a house. It doesn't have to be fancy, just be sure to include the major parts of any house. Label each room, and write how God would use that room to speak to you.

For example: in the living room, you might record that God wants to spend time with your entire family every day. Or that He wants you to feel free to crawl up in His lap every evening before you go to bed.

My Spiritual Floor Plan

A Prayer

Reminding Me To Be, Not Do

"And the Lord will deliver me from every evil work and preserve me for His heavenly kingdom. To Him be glory forever and ever. Amen!" (2 Timothy 4:18 NKJV).

Dear Lord, I come to You confessing the pride that has led me to this dark place. Somehow I've come to believe that if I don't control everything, the world around me will come crashing down. I've refused help when it's genuinely offered and taken on too much. Now I'm exhausted and frustrated, buried under so many responsibilities I was never meant to carry. And I have only myself to blame.

My unwillingness to let go and let others share this burden has threatened to destroy me. It's also affecting all those around me. They've quit asking if they can help, allowing me to continue to dig myself deeper into this pit of impossibility.

Only You can rescue me. Forgive me for what I've done that have led me here. I've been afraid to come to You, even though I know that You will meet me with love and forgiveness.

Help me swallow my pride and ask for the help I need from those who have offered in the past. Don't let them turn me down or berate me for not accepting their offers sooner. I don't deserve grace and mercy, but I know You don't give us what we deserve. You meet sorrow with love, pride with mercy, and repentance with open arms.

You are my salvation and my joy. Don't let me ever forget that again. Use this difficult time to remind me to draw close and concentrate on being, instead of doing. Amen.

A Devotion

Reminding Me that Balance and Confidence Go Together

"But blessed is the one who trusts in
the Lord, whose confidence is in him"
(Jeremiah 17:7 NIV).

We have three active sons—all grown. But
even now they haven't left behind their tendencies
toward reckless behavior. Beyond that, I'm always

amazed at their physical abilities. They rock climb and kayak. Play tennis and hike. They're also fond of something called slacklining.

Slacklining is an activity that refers to the act of walking or balancing along a suspended length of flat webbing that is strung between two anchors. It's similar to tightrope walking except it uses a different material and tension. Slacklines are strung loosely to create a surface that will stretch and bounce like a long and narrow trampoline.

My youngest son has an inflated idea of what I'm capable of and one day insisted on getting me up on his slackline. To his credit, he never once let go of my hand and was an excellent teacher. As he was giving me instruction, he said something that stuck with me. "Balance and confidence go together."

I discovered that—in regard to what he was teaching me that day—it was true. When I trusted him, I could balance better. But when I lost confidence, I began to wobble.

Later that phrase about balance and confidence continued to echo in my mind. As I considered where else the phrase was applicable, I was shocked to discover the idea stayed true in a lot of areas—particularly in my spiritual walk.

When I remain confident in Jesus' ability to guide my life, everything stays in balance. It doesn't matter what chaos surrounds me, He allows me to traverse life without wobbles or missteps. But when I

lose confidence—or rely on something uncertain—
everything comes crashing down.

I never did become proficient at slacklining, but
I'm learning daily to put my confidence in the One
who holds my hand.

Forging a Creative Connection

Let's play with the word BALANCE. We're going to use this word to construct another acrostic. But this time I want you to make a poem out of it. It doesn't have to rhyme, although it can if you prefer. You don't have to choose words that begin with each letter. Just make sure that each line of the poem contains the corresponding letter.

For example, the first line must contain a word with the letter B, the second line must contain a word with the letter A, etc.

After you've composed the poem, decorate the page with doodles, color, and any other creative expression that you wish.

A Prayer

About True Balance

"Therefore everyone who hears these words of Mine and acts on them, may be compared to a wise man who built his house on the rock" (Matthew 7:24 NASB).

Dear Lord, I desperately need a new definition for living a balanced life. I really thought balance meant everything was the same and life was calm. But that is not what my life looks like. I feel like I'm in a tiny boat in the midst of monster waves.

I'm being tossed this way and that and cannot do more than hang on. How can I have balance in the midst of chaos? I'm choosing to take a deep breath and quit looking at the waves and instead set my eyes on You.

You are the only place I can turn. I need an anchor. Your word promises me that I will find a foundation of peace that transcends my circumstances when I rely on You. Show me how You are working in my life right now.

Everything I count on has spiraled out of control. But I know nothing is beyond Your control. Not one single thing that's happened to me has taken You by surprise. Lead me to places in Your word that bring back my confidence in You. I always thought I was a woman of faith, but now I see I had a fair-weather type of faith.

I'm going to praise You for these circumstances and the way they're forcing me to learn what it really means to trust You. You are worthy of my trust and I know You are my rock and my deliverer. Amen.

3 Scripture Prescriptions to Meet God Where You Are

There are very few of us who wouldn't go see a doctor when we're ill. But for some reason, when our souls are ailing, we often avoid seeking out the recommendations of our heavenly physician. This list of Bible verses are what I like to term, Scripture prescriptions.

I recommend you decorate the verses and write what God is saying to you through each of them.

I also urge you to copy them onto index cards and tape them around your home and car. The constant reminder that God has an answer to what is wrong can bring us the peace we're so desperately craving.

"For I will satisfy the weary soul, and every languishing soul I will replenish" (Jeremiah 31:25 ESV).

"What then shall we say to these things? If God is for us, who is against us?" (Romans 8:31 NASB).

"Whoever dwells in the shelter of the Most High will rest in the shadow of the Almighty" (Psalm 91:1 NIV).

Chapter Five—*Moving On To Joy*

For me, the cure for weariness is more than rest. It's the resurgence of joy in my life. With joy comes renewed hope, energy, and much-needed renewal.

When we come out of a season of weariness, the first clue that we're leaving that place behind is the joy that begins to bubble up within us. I've learned that I can move from that place of exhaustion quicker if I'm purposefully cultivating joy.

Joy often starts its life as a seed. And like a seed, it's born in the inky blackness of pressure and heat. When I nurture that tiny seed, it finds the strength to push through darkness toward the light.

So how do we nurture the seed of joy? We help this seed grow by feeding it. Like any other seed, it needs loving care, the life-giving water of the Spirit, and plenty of Light to grow strong and blossom once again into the fullness.

This chapter will give us specifics on how to grow the joy in our lives from a tiny seed to a flowering plant.

To Remind Us that Joy Comes First

"Consider it all joy, my brethren, when you encounter various trials, knowing that the testing of your faith produces endurance. And let endurance have its perfect result, so that you may be perfect and complete, lacking in nothing" (James 1:2-4 NASB).

I used to get these verses out of order. As a matter fact, there was a time when I based my entire life-philosophy on an upside-down view of that passage.

My personality type is one that loves discipline and order. Add to that the sometimes overwhelming compulsion to control my world, and I had a recipe for disaster. I'd decided that the secret to a joyful life was found in the discipline of doing. But the more I tried to order my days and control everything around me, the further behind—and more unhappy—I became.

I added more programs to help me get organized. I searched for advice on being more disciplined. I tried every calendar and planner system known to man. Nothing helped. When the trials appeared, everything I was doing added to my stress instead of reducing it.

Finally I went back to the Bible. I searched for verses on joy and this section of James appeared. I almost didn't bother reading it because it was so familiar, but I felt a tug at my heart and turned to it. As I read, I began for the first time to see what it really said.

Joy comes first.

Then walking through the trials leads to the end result, becoming more like Christ.

I was going through the trials, trying to do everything else in the verse—having faith, continuing to persevere—and expecting the end result to be joy. But everything was harder when I didn't have the order right.

So now when a season of struggle comes, I start with joy. I look for good in the situation—what can I be thankful for—and build on those. It's not easy to do, but I can assure you it's life-changing.

Forging A Creative Connection

Today we're going to practice a physical expression of joy. I want you to turn on some music. Find some uplifting music, preferably praise music of some kind, and either use your ear buds or crank it up. Then I want you to move (dance) for the entire song. Raise your hands, clap, move your feet.

Now record what you experienced. You can write about it or draw something. You want to remember what you felt when you let go and practiced the joy of thanksgiving and praise.

My Feelings

A Prayer

To Help Me Choose Joy

"We also pray that you will be strengthened with all his glorious power so you will have all the endurance and patience you need. May you be filled with joy" (Colossians 1:11 NLT).

Dear Lord, I feel anything but joyful right now. I'm worn out, frustrated, and in that dark place of self-pity. I don't even want to search for reasons to be joyful, much less choose them.

I'm so tired of being in this place. I want to know that an end is in sight, yet I'm fearful about what that end looks like. Is it going to be another long tunnel of weariness?

As my exhaustion has increased, my hope has decreased. I'm not sure I'd even recognize joy if I found it. Help me find my way out of this weariness.

Decorate my days with moments of joy. Let me see the situation through Your eyes and recognize the good that's happening all around me. I know I'm not in a hopeless place, but I need You to guide me to see good.

Give me the opportunity to rest. I know that so much of my depression is caused by the fact that I'm so tired. Bring people into my life that will share this burden, then make me share—even if I resist their help.

Don't let me forget all that You've done for me in the past. Bring to mind the joy that You've gifted me with. Expand my sense of humor and give me reasons to laugh. You are the author of joy. Write that expression back into my life and show me how to once again choose joy. Amen.

A Devotion

To Remind Me that Detours Aren't Roadblocks

"A man's heart plans his way, but the Lord
determines his steps"
(Proverbs 16:9 HCSB).

I often miss the obvious. I used to look at any obstacle or detour in my path as a roadblock.

I've never met anyone who's road through life was a straight path. All of us have had times when reaching a goal or dream became a much longer journey than expected. So often our paths are filled with detours and odd twists. But one thing I can say is that each of those obstacles has been an important part of my journey, and I wouldn't be where I am today without the experience I gained along the way.

But I've also learned that those detours can bring us to a standstill, if we treat them like roadblocks.

I've had a lot of detours in my life. But one of the most difficult revolved around my publishing dreams and one of our sons.

I felt God's call to write for Him back in 1996. Ever since then I've been pursuing that dream. I succeeded with articles, blogs, and devotions but getting a book published wasn't something I was able to achieve, no matter how hard I tried. It seemed that God had built a roadblock for that particular part of my dream.

Then, in 2006, one of our sons chose to enlist in the military instead of attending college. We were button-busting proud of his decision to serve, but terrified of the sacrifice that service might require from him.

I spent the next few years struggling with fear as I sent him off twice on deployment to the Middle East. I wanted to quit and hide my head in the sand. I would have done almost anything to avoid that path as a parent.

I argued with God, bargained with God, and finally surrendered my son's well-being to God. It was a long—difficult—process, but the final result was peace.

Through this experience, I learned that every crossroad, every detour is a decision point. I could quit, or I could keep going. Ultimately it's that simple. During this difficult period, I continued to write.

The end result? First, and most important, our son is home safe and well. And also, on Veterans Day 2011 my first book debuted—a devotional for military families. It was by far the best first book I could have ever had because it was birthed out of the fire of experience. But I had to walk the path to get there. God hadn't erected roadblocks, He'd sent me on a detour that led me to the right time and place.

Take a look around you right now. You're in a unique place, a place that has a lot to teach you, a place you'll never be able to return to. Don't waste the experiences you have access to right now. Life rarely goes as planned, so it's time to get over that myth. Enjoy the journey and embrace the process. Go deep and wide, and no matter what the future brings you'll have be on the right path.

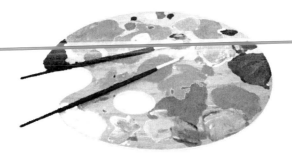

Forging A Creative Connection

Draw two footprints. You can trace your shoe, or wing it, doesn't matter. In one footprint, write out Jeremiah 29:11. In the other one, write a Bible verse of your choice that reminds you that God is in control of your path.

Standing on the Word of God

A Prayer

For You to Direct My Path Through This Tangled Time

"Seek his will in all you do, and he will
show you which path to take"
(Proverbs 3:6 NLT).

Dear Lord, this is such a difficult time right now. I can't seem to see more than a step or two in any direction. All the paths open to me seem to lead into a tangled mess. Don't let me choose wrongly.

Every step seems to be landing in sinking mud and my forward motion is slow and difficult. Moving forward is exhausting, and I'm discouraged. Show me which way to go.

You and You alone know the beginning from the end. My guess at what to do next or which place to place my foot is worthless. Be my guide through this set of circumstances.

I know You have only the best in mind for me, but I can't see it. I can sense that it's close, but now I'm afraid that if I choose the wrong path, I'll miss it. Be my guide and my certainty in this place.

I know it's been said that it's darkest before the dawn. I want to believe that. I want to see how this experience will strengthen my faith. But I'm tired and my faith seems weak and like it won't last long enough to get me through this.

Shine Your light here and illuminate my path. Reach down and carry me through this boggy place. Return my joy and bolster my faith so I may tell others of the work You've done in my life. Make me a beacon of hope because of Your faithfulness. Amen.

A Devotion

To Remind Me That I Can't Do This Alone

"Two are better than one, because they
have a good return for their labor: If either
of them falls down, one can help the other
up. But pity anyone who falls and has no
one to help them up"
(Ecclesiastes 4:9-10 NIV).

While I've been blessed with some amazing
friends, I'm not the type who makes close friends
easily. I tend to be the type of person who naturally
isolates, especially when living gets tough.

191

Just like a lion singles out his prey, separating it from the herd, so stress and weariness can separate us from any support we may have. I'm not a people person, and when I'm insecure, hurting or scared, I crawl in a hole and disappear. My retreat just adds to the problem.

During a difficult time I retreated—away from friends and those who could help. This time, instead of leaving me to my own devices, two friends came after me. They noticed my withdrawal and began calling and texting. At first, I answered their messages, assuring them I was fine. But when they persisted, I ignored their outreach.

These dear sisters just wouldn't take no for an answer. One evening they showed up on my doorstep. With my husband's encouragement, they whisked me off to dinner and a girl's night out. Sure enough, my worst fears were realized. I broke down sobbing during the meal. Instead of being embarrassed or upset, they let me cry. Then together, the three of us tackled the struggles I'd been trying to face alone.

We didn't come up with earth-shattering answers, but I discovered a profound peace and strength in knowing I was no longer alone. They stuck by me as I walked out that tough time. And I've done the same thing for other friends who retreated when life got hard.

I learned that God doesn't want us to cope alone. He is always with us, and He often sends others to be His physical representation during difficult times. It's only when I reach up—to God, and then out—to those He's put in my life to encourage me, I grow stronger.

Forging A Creative Connection

Today I want you to take a few minutes and write a letter to a friend. Choose someone who has been there for you recently. Tell them how much their support has meant to you and how you see their friendship as a gift from God.

Write the letter in the space below and on the next page first, then copy it into a card and mail or hand deliver the letter to your friend.

A Letter to a Friend

A Prayer

Asking You to Give Me Traveling Companions

"For where two or three are gathered in my
name, there am I among them"
(Matthew 18:20 ESV).

Dear Lord, You are my ever present help in
times of trouble. But on this difficult journey, I'm also
asking You to give me traveling companions. I know

the value of friendship, but I've been too weary to nurture that kind of friendship and now I need Your help. Send some friends to help me navigate the circumstances I'm going through right now.

In addition to being exhausted, I'm also tired of being alone. I crave someone to come alongside me and provide the encouragement to finish strong. I want to know that someone else understands what I've been going through.

I don't need someone to carry me through, only someone to share my thoughts and fears. Even as I search for a band of fellow travelers, I pray that You keep me from those who would be false friends. Don't let me chose companions who will lead me astray.

Use me to encourage others in this group. When one stumbles make us quick to stop and lift her up. Don't allow any of us to develop a heart of judgment or condemnation. Instead, give me steady friends who will remind me of all the truths You've taught me. Knit us together and let us challenge one another to greater faith and a deeper understanding of who You are. Amen.

A Devotion

Reminding Me of What Knot to Do

"For I know the plans that I have for you,'
declares the LORD, 'plans for welfare and
not for calamity to give you a future and a
hope" (Jeremiah 29:11 NASB).

I met several friends for coffee the other day
and of course, I took my knitting with me. For some
reason it's impossible for me to sit still—my hands
have to be busy for my mind to be calm. Usually
knitting it the activity I choose to help me relax.

As we went back and forth, discussing our days one of my friends mentioned how neatly my ball of yarn was behaving. It should have been, I'd spent hours winding that particular fiber.

My friend, also a knitter, shared how she'd been in a hurry to start a recent project and hadn't bothered to wind her yarn into a ball. Instead she took the risk of leaving it in a loose skein. Anyone who's ever tried to save time this way knows what happened to her next—a knot of hopelessly tangled yarn.

We all shared a sympathetic laugh as she explained the lengths she'd had to go to unsnarl the mess. Instead of saving time, she'd spent many more hours just trying to get started again. As she regaled us with what she'd had to do to get her yarn back into some kind of manageable state, another woman at the table drew a comparison I'll never forget. "Isn't that like life? When we get in a hurry and rush ahead of God, life ends up in a tangled knot."

Oh the wisdom in that insight. It certainly made me pause. Now, whenever I get impatient with God's timing and consider rushing ahead, I visualize the snarled mess that's likely to occur. Instead I take a deep breath and keep waiting as I let God order my days, return my joy and remember what KNOT to do.

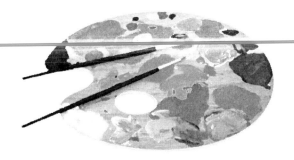

Forging a Creative Connection

Copy this verse in the blank space:
"A person standing alone can be attacked and defeated, but two can stand back-to-back and conquer. Three are even better, for a triple-braided cord is not easily broken" (Ecclesiastes 4:12 NLT).

Now, using string, yarn, or ribbon, measure and cut nine pieces—each one eighteen inches long. Hold three pieces together at a time and tie a knot in one end. Braid the three pieces together and again knot the end. Repeat with the remaining six pieces. You should end up with three braided cords.

While you're braiding, say a prayer. Ask God to bring you two other friends to make a cord of three prayer partners.

Record the names of the friends He brought to mind. Contact each one and ask if they'd like to become part of your three-person prayer team. When one says yes, give them one of the cords. Keep one cord for yourself and use it as a bookmark for your Bible or current journal.

My Three Friends

A Prayer

Of Hope for Tomorrow

"Now faith is confidence in what we hope for and assurance about what we do not see" (Hebrews 11:1 NIV).

Dear Lord, this has been a difficult time in my life. I've been weary in ways I never imagined. I've shouldered responsibilities I never asked for.

I've learned that stumbling isn't failure, and those who endure truly will find joy again. Through all of this You've been my sustainer and my constant companion.

Although I'm still battling, I can see the light at the end of the tunnel. And my joy has returned.

Don't let me waste the lessons I've learned during this season. Use them to encourage me when trying times come again. Even more than that, use them to encourage others.

Let me be Your example of how great a work You can do through an unworthy vessel. Don't let anyone make the mistake of believing that it was my strength or wisdom that got me through this. Instead show them Your glory and how much You love each of us.

It has been only through You that I've come through this. When the weariness threatened to drive me from Your presence, You came searching. You sent others to help me carry the burdens of this time. They also spoke words that uplifted me and pointed me back to You.

To say I'm grateful is the most inadequate use of language. You are my all in all. You love me in ways I never imagined, and You've proven You'll never leave me or forsake me. Give me opportunities to tell others of how You've worked in my life. And never let me forget what I've experienced through these challenging days and nights. Amen.

A Devotion

About the Treasures Found in Difficult Times

"I will give you hidden treasures, riches
stored in secret places, so that you may
know that I am the Lord, the God of Israel,
who summons you by name."
(Isaiah 45:3 NIV).

We all want our lives to matter. We want God to use us to touch hearts, change lives, challenge the status quo. We strive to walk closely with God and rejoice when He accomplishes big victories. But what if the treasure we're searching for isn't only found in the victories. What if there are also gems buried in our troubles?

Mining is hard work, and as I recently looked at a miner's tools of the trade, I found some interesting parallels that helped me see gold in places I'd once thought only dark pits of failure.

Miners of old wielded heavy pick axes and bulky shovels. They built sluice boxes and patiently plied gold pans looking for nuggets. This was necessary because the treasure was often buried under hard rock and hidden amongst worthless mud.

I found the same type of obstacles when I dug through my past experiences. I found treasures buried, not under tons of rock, but beneath rock-hard walls I'd erected between me and the pain in my past. When I began to actually look for treasure, I also spotted gold closer to the surface—hidden in plain sight beside everyday occurrences. These gems were often camouflaged to look worthless but were valuable nuggets of inspiration. Miners—then and now—are often easy to spot because of their attire. From the metal hard hats, with attached lights, to the tips of their steel-toed boots, everything about them is geared to plying their trade.

I found that when I began mining my past difficulties I also needed protection for my mind as the emotions of past failures came hurtling at my mind like rain of heavy stones. My feet also had to be shod in a foundation of who I am. I needed that protection when I went mucking around in the dangerous mine shafts of yesterday. Even the good memories can hold dangers, deceiving us and seducing us into what-might-have-been.

The light I needed was the focus of what I was searching for—the point of those events. I had to have the light of God's truth illuminate those past happenings. Otherwise I could wander into a side-tunnel and get lost forever.

God taught me that each of us has a unique set of life experiences. Our lives are a convergence of time and space, and comprised of people and experiences. He's showing me the value of what's gone before. I'm learning not to waste what God has allowed.

Forging a Creative Connection

I am directionally challenged. I not only find it difficult to navigate a physical path, but I also struggle staying on the path that God has for me. But there is one thing that has helped me discern the spiritual path. And that is by using spiritual markers.

Early in our marriage, a wise pastor advised that instead of making New Year's resolutions, we instead look back at the spiritual markers we had in the previous year. This discipline has led us to take note of what we might have otherwise missed.

I've adapted this practice when I'm faced with a difficult season of life. When God seems far away or life is chaotic in the extreme, I pull out a piece of paper and begin to list all God has done or said. Then I connect the dots. I write out the ways one thing has led to another and before long, I can once again see the path. Today you're going to give this a try.

Finding Your Spiritual Markers

First, think back to something major you remember God doing in your life or saying to you. It could be a time when you gave your testimony, or witnessed to someone. It could be a moment when someone affirmed a calling you felt God had put on your life. You might choose to begin with a Bible verse you read where you heard God speak into the silence of your soul. The time frame isn't important. You could go back years or only a few months. Pray and ask God where He wants you to start, then begin there.

Next, think about where that first thing led you. What was the next time you felt God's Spirit moving around or through you? Record what you remember.

Now find two or three more instances of when God revealed something to you.

Finally, connect these events and write out where you think God is leading you. Don't be afraid of something too big or something too small. God works in ways we cannot image. His ways are not our ways. Don't limit Him. Let Him speak and then, write it down.

My Spiritual Markers

A Prayer

About My Treasure

"For where your treasure is, there your heart will be also" (Luke 12:34 NASB).

Dear Lord, I've been thinking a lot about what's important in life. Walking through this difficult season has caused a shift in my priorities. I don't think that's a bad thing. I was spending so much time and energy on the unimportant.

But now that I'm aware of the changes I still need to make, I'm locked in battle with my old to-do list. I don't want to go back. I want to take the lessons I've learned and move forward into a deeper—more satisfying—walk with You.

Help me cement those new priorities in such a way that I'm no longer tempted to by the old. Remind me of the joy I feel when I focus on You, and the relationships of those You've put in my life.

Don't let me revert to acting like I'm responsible for the impossible. You are the miracle worker, not me. I never want to put myself in Your place again. You've given me such treasures—those I love, the blessings of my life today, and especially the relationship with You. Don't let me trade value for worthless junk.

You are all I need. Remind me of this place and time when the busyness of life tries to crowd in. Never let me forget the gift of walking with You. Amen.

3 Scripture Prescriptions to Meet God Where You Are

Few of us wouldn't go see a doctor when we're ill. But for some reason, when our souls are ailing, we often avoid seeking out the recommendations of our heavenly physician. This list of Bible verses are what I like to term, Scripture prescriptions.

I recommend you decorate the verses and write what God is saying to you through each of them.

I also urge you to copy them onto index cards and tape them around your home and car. The constant reminder that God has an answer to what is wrong can bring us the peace we're so desperately craving.

"Now may the God of hope fill you with
all joy and peace as you believe in Him so
that you may overflow with hope by the
power of the Holy Spirit"
(Romans 15:13 HCSB).

"Those who plant in tears will harvest with
shouts of joy" (Psalm 126:5 NLT).

"So also you have sorrow now, but I will
see you again, and your hearts will rejoice,
and no one will take your joy from you"
(John 16:22 ESV).

About the Author

Edie Melson

Find your voice, live your story...is the foundation of Edie Melson's message, no matter if she's reaching readers, parents, military families, or writers. As an author, blogger, and speaker she's encouraged and challenged audiences across the country and around the world. Her numerous books reflect her passion to help others develop the strength of their God-given gifts and apply them to their lives.

In addition to being a writer, Edie has this to say, "I'm creative out of self-defense. As the daughter of an artist-mother and musician-turned-photographer-father, I'd have been a disgrace if I hadn't been true to my creativity." Edie also dabbles in photography, bullet journaling, and knitting.

Edie's a popular speaker and a board member of the Advanced Writers and Speakers Association, You can find her blogging regularly on www.Soulfulink.com, www.AriseDaily.com, and Just18Summers.com. Connect with her on her website, www.EdieMelson.com and through Instagram, Twitter, and Facebook.